The Timetraveller's Guide to . . .

SAXON AND VIKING LONDON

Joshua Doder

WATLING STREET

Joshua Doder lives in London with his wife, two dogs, three cats and a ferret called Miki. He has worked as a chef, a librarian and an actor. His hobbies include collecting Japanese pottery and climbing mountains. He is now writing a short history of pizza.

The Timetraveller's
Guide to . . .

SAXON *and* VIKING
LONDON

First published in 2004 by Watling St Publishing
The Glen
Southrop
Lechlade
Gloucestershire
GL7 3NY

Printed in Italy

ISBN 1-904153-07-0

24681097531

Design: Mackerel Limited
Illustrations: Mark Davis

www.tempus-publishing.com

Contents

INTRODUCTION

Close your eyes and try to imagine what London looks like.

Okay, you can open your eyes now.

What did you see in your imagination?

I'll tell you what I see if I close my eyes and imagine what London looks like: I see bricks and glass and tarmac. I see big buildings. I see lots of cars. I see thousands of people hurrying through the streets. I see noise and bustle. There is one thing that unites everything in my imaginary picture of London: all of it has been created by human beings, and nothing is natural.

When the Saxons and Vikings lived in London, things were very different. There were very few roads or buildings. There weren't many people either. Humanity had not made its mark on the landscape.

Where London is today, there was a huge expanse of dense forests, divided by a few muddy roads and a handful of villages. The river was much wider than it is now. The land was wet and swampy. Thick forests stretched to the horizon. Shadows darted through the trees – the sparrows and eagles, foxes and wild boars. If you walked for a few minutes through the forest, you would  probably get completely lost. If you were lucky, you would eventually find your way back to your village. If you were very unlucky, you might meet a bear, who would tear you to pieces and leave your body for the crows to eat.

A Warning

You will find many interesting things in this book. Some of them probably aren't true.

Not true? Why not?

For one simple reason: because historians don't know much about the Dark Ages – which is what people call the time that the Saxons and the Vikings ruled England. As you will discover in this book, historians have a hard time making any decisions about Saxon and Viking London. The Saxons and Vikings didn't write many books. They didn't build many buildings. And they lived a long, long time ago.

So, a lot of the facts in this book probably aren't true – but they might not be false either. They are good guesses. Using clues left by the Saxons and the Vikings, archaeologists and historians have tried to guess how Saxon and Viking London might have looked. They might be right – but they might be wrong.

8

The Lonely Figure of the Archaeologist

Here you can see a picture of an archaeologist. You will notice certain distinguishing features.

Firstly, he has an absent-minded and bemused expression. This is because he spends all his time worrying about the past, and doesn't have much space in his mind left for things like lunch and where he put his socks. Secondly, he is carrying a paintbrush. Archaeologists have to be very careful not to damage the ancient objects that they dig out of the earth, so they don't use shovels; they use brushes, and gently scrape the earth away from  whatever they are digging up. Thirdly, he is holding a magnifying glass. This allows him to inspect all the interesting objects that he finds, and use them to build a picture of how people lived in the past.

As you must be able to see, he is a lonely and confused man. He spends his life digging very carefully in the dirt and dust, trying to discover the truth about our ancestors. All the time, other people are trying to foil him: they want to build new roads, new houses, new offices, new railway tracks, new airports, and bury the past under thick piles of new steel and new concrete.

In modern London, the builders and the archaeologists have made a deal. When a new building is going to be built, the builders wait for a little time until the archaeologists have looked at the site. The archaeologists remove any interesting material, take it to their laboratories and study it. They look at the earth, and discover how the old streets looked. They find the ancient foundations of houses. They recreate how the city used to look.

By the time that the builders start building, all the antiques from the earth will have been transferred to a museum – like the Museum of London, for instance – where you and I can look at them.

Q Why were the Dark Ages called the Dark Ages?

A) Because electricity hadn't been invented yet, so it was really dark.

B) Because the sun didn't rise for seven hundred years.

C) Because people didn't write much down, so historians don't know very much about the period.

Answer: C) is, strangely, the correct answer. However, over the past few years, historians have discovered more and more about the Darks Ages. Now, historians don't even call them the Dark Ages any more. They talk about 'Late Antiquity' or 'Pre-Medieval Times.'

CHAPTER ONE

The End of the Romans

Who are Londoners?

That's a pretty simple question, you might think. They are people who live in London.

Okay, here's a more complicated question. Who are the English? And another complicated question. Who are the British?

Are they the people who live in England? Or the people who live in Britain?

11

What about a Frenchman who leaves Paris and comes to live in London. Is he English? Is he British? Is he a Londoner?

What about a German or a Dane or a Swede who leaves Berlin or Copenhagen or Stockholm and comes to live in London? Are they English? Are they British? Are they Londoners?

In the time of the Saxons and the Vikings, this is exactly what happened. People came from all over Europe, and settled here. At first, they fought one another. Then, they lived together. Gradually, they all mingled together. Now, we can't tell them apart.

The first Saxons started arriving in Britain in about the fifth century. They came from Germany. They arrived with weapons and horses and ploughs, determined to find new homes for themselves.

The Romans

Two thousand years ago, a huge empire stretched over the whole of Europe and North Africa. The Romans ruled an expanse of land which stretched from Egypt in the south-east to Scotland in the north-west.

Around the year AD 400 (in other words, four hundred years after the birth of Jesus Christ), the Roman Empire came under threat from an army of wild-eyed, hairy men and women called the Goths. The Romans liked central heating, swimming pools and hard work. The Goths liked burning down houses, killing little furry animals and stealing other people's money. As you can imagine, the Romans and the Goths weren't the best of friends.

To escape from the Goths, the Romans withdrew to their capital, Rome, leaving the distant corners of their empire to fend for themselves. All those countries which had been ruled by the Romans suddenly became free to do whatever they liked. They didn't have to obey Roman laws or pay taxes to the Romans. They didn't have to believe in Roman gods or eat Roman food. They didn't have to listen to Roman jokes or sing Roman songs. They were free!

This book covers the years from the end of the Roman occupation of Britain to the beginning of the Norman occupation of Britain. In other words, I shall describe the years between the Romans leaving and the Normans arriving.

The Romans left in AD 407. The Normans arrived in 1066. Between those years, London was occupied by the Angles, the Saxons and the Vikings. Work it out for yourself: how many years elapsed between the Romans leaving and the Normans arriving? Clue: the answer is 1066 minus 407.

(Editor's Note: If you want to discover more about Roman London why not… plug plug…buy a copy of *The Timetraveller's Guide to Roman London* also published by Watling Street – see the back of this book for more details!)

EXCHANGIOUS AND MARTUS

TOGAS FOR SALE

Four Lovely Togas for Sale.
Any decent offer will be
considered. Sale due to
re-location – we are
returning to Rome, and
our British togas will
simply be too hot for the
Roman sunshine.

Also available: three
bear skins, various pots
and pans, two spears, a
dagger (slightly chipped)
and one chariot, two years
old, hardly used, brand
new left-hand wheel.

Apply to Centurion Marcus Antonius at the Legion House.

The Decline and Fall of the Roman Empire

In the last days of the Roman Empire, the Romans had grown
tired of fighting. They preferred to eat grapes, drink wine and
write poetry. So, they hired other people to do their fighting for
them. When you hire a soldier to fight for you, he is called a
mercenary. In Britain, the Romans hired lots of German
mercenaries. The Germans were famous for being hairy, tall and
excellent fighters.

However, the Romans soon realised that they had made a big mistake by hiring all these German mercenaries. The mercenaries rebelled. Some ran away. Others turned round and started fighting against the Romans.

In the year AD 407, the Romans threw up their hands, climbed into their ships, and sailed back to France. They didn't like Britain. They hated the weather, the food and the savages who lived there.

After the Romans?

With the Romans gone, new people began to settle in England – they can be divided into five separate tribes: the Britons, the Angles, the Saxons, the Fresians and the Jutes. The Britons had been living in Britain for centuries already. The Angles and Saxons came from  Angeln and Saxony (both now in modern Germany). The Fresians came from modern Holland and the Jutes came from Jutland (now in modern Denmark).

Over the next few years, more and more Saxons, Jutes, Fresians and Angles arrived in Britain. They didn't invade in an organised army; instead, a few of them came every year. Maybe some of them came on holiday, and decided not to go home again. Others might have gone fishing in a boat, and got lost on the sea. Still more probably just fancied a bit of a change.

Some of the Britons didn't like their new neighbours, and went to live in Wales, Cornwall or Brittany (a bit of France that is called after all the Britons who lived there). Other Britons stayed where they were. As you can imagine, it was all pretty complicated. People got jumbled together. They fought one another, traded with one another, married one another and ended up living together.

Now, hundreds of years later, you can't tell who is an Angle and who is a Jute, who is a Briton and who is a Saxon. All of them are mixed together. The only trace of the different tribes can be found in the names: England is named after the Angles and Britain is named after the Britons.

CHAPTER TWO

Lundenwic

Today, people often say that London isn't a real city. Instead, they say, it is a collection of joined-up villages.

Each village, these people claim, has an individual character which is quite different from the other villages in London. If you walk through Hampstead Village, for instance, you could never imagine that you were in Dulwich Village. Although only a few minutes in a car separates Brixton, Stockwell and Clapham, you could never get them confused.

If you live in London, you probably know which village you live in. Your village probably has its own post office, its own shops, and, most importantly, its own character, entirely different from any of the other villages in the city. And yet, all these villages are part of London.

The Saxons could have lived in the city built by the Romans. It was sitting there: a smart old city with tall solid stone walls and lots of sturdy houses which would withstand even in the biggest storm. However, the Saxons chose not to live in the old Roman city.

When the Romans had gone, people avoided London. The city remained unoccupied. No one bothered building a bridge over the Thames for two hundred years.

Perhaps the Saxons thought that a few pesky Romans might still be living inside the walls, doing all the sneaky stuff that Romans do like drinking wine and inventing central heating. Or perhaps they just didn't like the smell left by the Romans. You might have thought that the smell might have faded after a few years, but the Saxons had very sensitive noses. Rather than living in the Roman city, they preferred to live in lots of little villages, spread round the countryside. They settled in Uxbridge, Enfield, Islington and Vauxhall. They built small, self-enclosed villages with fences and barricades to protect themselves from intruders and invaders. They kept themselves to themselves, and didn't interfere in the lives of the other nearby villages.

If you don't like the way that London is divided into villages, you should blame the Saxons.

Pick Wic

Have you ever been shopping in Covent Garden? Or visited the Royal Opera House? If you have, you will have walked over the site of Lundenwic, where the Saxons lived for hundreds of years.

Until the 1980s, no one knew that Lundenwic had ever existed. Historians and archaeologists who thought about Saxon London spent a lot of time scratching their heads. They couldn't find much evidence of the Saxons in the old Roman city, or anywhere else. But they were looking in the wrong place. They assumed that the Saxons would have lived in the same part of the city as the Romans. In fact, the Saxons chose to live somewhere quite different.

In the 1990s, the Opera House in Covent Garden was completely rebuilt. Underneath the building, a group of archaeologists discovered something amazing: the remains of Saxon London. They found pots, daggers, bones and a street with sixty houses. They now think that the Saxon town stretched all the way from Covent Garden to Oxford Street. Rather than using the Roman name 'Londinium', the Saxons called their city 'Lundenwic'.

To the Saxons, the word wic meant market or port. During Saxon times, the biggest trading towns in England were Hamwic (now called Southampton), Gippeswic (now called Ipswich) and Lundenwic (now called London). There are other places in England which have taken their names from the Saxon name for a port: for instance, you might know Sandwich and Fordwich in Kent and Greenwich in East London.

The name 'Lundenwic' still exists in modern London, although it has changed over the past few centuries. Do you know a street named Aldwych? It is a large, busy road near Covent Garden. Over the past thousand years 'Lundenwic' has evolved into 'Aldwych.' If you go to the shops, the theatre or the opera in Covent Garden, you really are walking directly above the site of the biggest Saxon settlement in London!

London has changed almost unbelievably over the past two thousand years. If a Saxon or a Viking suddenly arrived in modern London, he wouldn't be able to believe his eyes. However, there are many, many connections between modern London and all the people who have lived in the city over the centuries. The names of streets are just one way that you can see these connections.

The Town Where Snot Lived

Many places in Britain were named by the Saxons and the Vikings, and their names have not changed since. Nowadays, most people don't know what the names mean. This is probably a good thing. For instance, the citizens of Nottingham must be delighted that no one remembers where their city got its name.

Nottingham means 'Snot's ham.' In other words, it means 'the place where Snot and his family live.' In Saxon times, there was an important warrior named Snot who lived there.

Over the years, the 's' fell out of the name, and Snot has been forgotten. If you ever meet anyone from Nottingham, you can tell them that you know the truth about their city: it was founded by a man named Snot.

Trading Places

Lundenwic means 'London the port' or 'London the market.' The city was the centre of trade in England. All along the riverbank, merchants built barns and houses to store their goods. Ships docked on the shore to load up. Farmers brought animals, food and wool from their farms to sell. At the same time, craftsmen started working in London, because they could easily sell their produce to the city's merchants.

From London, sailors and merchants travelled all around Britain and Europe. The bravest sailed even further. In those days, most people still believed that the world was flat – so you had to be very brave to go on a long sea voyage. You never knew when you might reach the end of the world and fall off.

The Saxons had wine from France, silks from India and spices from China. We know this from the work of archaeologists. When archaeologists dig up sites in London, they find all kinds of interesting bits and pieces from all around the world. For instance, when archaeologists find Arabic coins in London, they know that the Saxons either traded with Arab merchants or stole the coins from someone who had.

CHAPTER THREE

Inside a Saxon House

After the Romans left Britain and the Saxons arrived, there wasn't one king ruling the country. There weren't even two kings who divided the country between them. There were HUNDREDS of kings ruling over different parts of the country, each of them guarding his territory from the other kings and imposing his wishes on his subjects. None of them wanted to be ordered around by anyone else. All of them said, 'I'm the king, and I'll do what I like!'

'No, you're not. I'm the king! And I'll do whatever I like!'

'Oh, will you?'

'Yes, I will, actually.'

'We'll soon see about that. Do you see this big, sharp sword? Do what I say, or I'll chop your head off.'

'Okay, okay. You're the king.'

Conversations like that happened up and down the country for a few hundred years. Some kings surrendered gracefully, and admitted that they weren't really kings after all. Others insisted on fighting. Over the centuries, the two hundred kingdoms merged together. It was inconvenient having so many kings in one country. By the time of King Alfred, only two kings ruled different parts of England.

Just as the country was ruled by a king, so the village was ruled by a lord. He was the richest and most powerful man in the village. The lord had a sword and a horse. He lived in the biggest building in the village – usually called the Great Hall. Directly below him were people called free men. If you were a free man, you didn't belong to anyone. You probably fought with a spear rather than a sword. You lived in your own house. You worked for the lord, and he paid you with money or a share of the crop.

The lowliest people in the village were the slaves. They owned nothing, not even a knife. A slave would live wherever he could, and do whatever he was told to do. The Saxons and Vikings believe that one person could be owned by another. If you were my slave, I would own you, just as I owned a cow, a pig or a horse. If I felt like it, I could sell you or even kill you, and no one would care.

As a slave, you could earn your freedom. Your master might decide to free you if you had worked very hard, or saved his life, or earned his gratitude in some other way. The act of freeing a slave is called manumission.

Bored Games

Life for the Saxons was slow, cold and boring.

You might think that things haven't changed much. If so, think of some of the differences between your life and the life of a child in a Saxon village. Have you been in an aeroplane? Or a car? Or ridden a bicycle? Saxons didn't know what any of those things were. Have you ever eaten a burger? Or washed your clothes in a washing-machine? Or watched TV? Or listened to the radio? Saxons didn't have any of those things.

During the long, dark nights in the winter, when the snow lay on the ground and the candles spluttered, giving off hardly any light, the Saxons would amuse themselves by playing games. Here are some of the games that they played:

DICE. Saxon dice were the same as modern dice – but they were made from a deer's antlers rather than plastic. The game of dice hasn't changed at all in the past fifteen hundred years: you take turns to throw the dice, and the winner is the person who gets the highest score.

BOARD GAMES. The Saxons had simple board games such as NOUGHTS AND CROSSES and NINE MEN'S MORRIS. They didn't have more complicated games like chess and draughts.

RIDDLING. The Saxons loved riddles. They sat around the fire, inventing clever riddles for other people to guess. Here is a very simple Saxon riddle:

'In the morning, I am rock. In the afternoon, I am water. In the night, I am rock again. What am I?'

Answer: ice. Now, see if you can make up a riddle of your own.

Saxon Style

The Saxons had simple clothes. Men and women wore woollen smocks. A woman's smock stretched to the ground like a long dress. A man's smock would reach his waist, like a simple shirt, and he would wear trousers underneath it. Everyone wore a belt around their waists.

Your important personal possessions – a knife, keys, money – would hang from your belt. Wealthy women wore some jewellery – a necklace, some bracelets, a brooch. In the winter, you would wear a cloak to keep out the cold. If you were lucky, you would have a thick animal skin to wrap around your shoulders.

Safe as Houses

Each of the Saxon villages in London looked alike: each one had its own defences, a deep ditch and a wooden fence around the boundary to stop animals running away and prevent enemies just walking in. Outside the fence, they grew crops in fields. Inside the fence, they built houses.

The houses were built of wood. They had only one storey, and most had just one room. Inside, a fire burnt day and night, and food bubbled in a pot. People had very little furniture – maybe a table and some benches, maybe nothing at all. Mostly, people sat on the floor, and slept there too. In the winter, they covered themselves with animal skins and huddled together for warmth.

Tapestries hung on the walls to keep out the cold. The roof was made of mud and thatch. As you can imagine, the houses weren't very strong. Fierce rain would wash the mud from the roof, letting water into the house. A strong wind might blow the house down. After a big storm, most people in the village had to rebuild their homes.

The Saxons were amazed by Roman buildings, which were made out of stone. The Romans had running water in their homes, and some of their houses even had a primitive form of central heating. Perhaps that is one of the reasons that the Saxons chose not to live in Roman London: they might have thought that the Romans were magicians.

Money, Money, Money

The Saxons used pounds, shillings and pence. If you ask your parents or your grandparents, you will discover that they used pounds, shillings and pence too. This doesn't mean that they lived in Saxon times. The system of Saxon money continued in Britain until 1971.

A Saxon pound was a pound of silver. If you bought something for five pounds, you wouldn't hand over five little coins – you would have to carry a big bag of silver, weighing five pounds (roughly two and a half kilograms).

A pound was divided into twenty shillings, and each shilling was divided into twelve pennies. So, there were two hundred and forty pennies in a pound. Here is a rough idea of how much things would cost:

One chicken – 1 penny

One lamb – 6 pennies

One pig – 20 pennies

A well-trained dog – 120 pennies

A slow, old horse – 60 pennies

A fast, young horse – 200 pennies

1 pound of corn – 1 penny

A knife – 2 pennies

A sword – 100 pennies

A spear – 80 pennies

A shield – 40 pennies

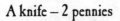

Quiz

1) If you had two pounds, how many chickens could you buy?

2) If you wanted to buy two well-trained dogs, twenty chickens and three pigs and a fast horse, how much money would you need?

3) If you wanted to buy a sword, two spears, a shield and a fast horse, how much money would you need?

Answers: 1) four hundred and eighty chickens; 2) 520 pennies which is two pounds and forty pennies; 3) 500 pennies.

You've just killed my dad!

That will be two hundred shillings, please!

The Saxons had primitive laws. Rather than prison, they used a system called wergild. If you killed someone, you had to pay his family. How much you paid depended on the person's importance.

If you killed a king, you had to pay 8,000 shillings.

If you killed an earl, you had to pay eight hundred shillings. You might have to pay a bit more if he owned a lot of land, or a bit less if he wasn't very important.

If you killed a freeman, you had to pay two hundred shillings.

If you killed a slave, you didn't have to pay anything. The Saxons thought that slaves were worthless.

If you didn't have enough money to pay the wergild, your punishment would be even worse: you would stop being an earl or a freeman, and become a slave. Then anyone could kill you for free.

CHAPTER FOUR

Finding Food

Today, London is a huge, sprawling city, covered with buildings. There are some trees and patches of grass, but they are overwhelmed by man-made objects – houses, offices, cars, roads, railway tracks and so on. For the Saxons and the Vikings, the opposite was true. Man did not dominate nature. Nature dominated man.

When the Saxons lived in London, the river Thames was much wider than it is now. The land was wet and swampy. Thick forests stretched to the horizon. If you walked for a few minutes through the forest, you would probably get completely lost, and you might never find your way back to your village. There were no signposts and few houses. Wild animals roamed through the forest: bears, foxes, wolves and wild boar. All of them would be happy to eat you.

Saxon Supper versus Modern Menu

What would you rather eat? And which is healthier?

THE MODERN MENU

MAIN COURSE
Cheeseburger with fries

PUDDING
Strawberry ice cream

DRINK
Chocolate milkshake

THE SAXON SUPPER

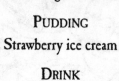

MAIN COURSE
Roast squirrel sandwich

Salad of carrots, marigold
flowers and dandelion leaves

PUDDING
Fresh strawberries,
raspberries and blackberries

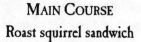

DRINK
Glass of water

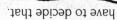

Answer: the Saxon Supper is much, much healthier than the Modern Menu. As for which you would rather eat – well, you'll have to decide that.

32

Plants grew everywhere. The Saxons had few farms and no shops. When they wanted some food, they wandered into the forest, and gathered whatever they could find.

Nowadays, we make a strict distinction between edible plants and inedible plants – in other words, betweens plants that you can eat and plants that you can't eat. We eat plants that we buy in shops and supermarkets, but we don't eat plants that are just growing in the fields, the woods, the garden or beside the road.

The Saxons weren't so strict. They ate a plant if it tasted good. In fact, they probably ate a plant even if it tasted bad, just as long as it wasn't poisonous. The Saxons definitely ate lots of plants that we would describe as weeds: in their salads, they would eat dandelion, dock, rocket, mustard, fennel, marigold, campion, lettuce and poppy leaves. We still eat some of these plants in our salads today; others, we grow in the garden for their flowers.

Just as they ate some peculiar plants, the Saxons and Vikings ate all kinds of meat that might make us feel sick. They would cook squirrels, hedgehogs, rats and mice. They would catch seagulls, pigeons and sparrows, and barbecue them over a hot fire. If they were very hungry, they would even eat horses, cats and dogs, although they preferred not to.

There was one animal that the Saxons and Vikings would never eat however hungry they might have been. That was human meat. Cannibalism (which means eating creatures of the same species as yourself) was strictly forbidden by both the Saxons and the Vikings.

Feast and Fast

A typical Saxon meal was very simple. You started with bread and vegetables. You finished with fruit. And that was it. On special days, like someone's birthday or a religious holiday, you would have meat or fish. If the chickens had been laying well, you might have a boiled egg. But most people just ate bread and vegetables. Bread was an essential part of every meal, and a vital part of life. You could pay for things using bread rather than money.

To make things more interesting, people would feast and fast. For a feast, you ate a lot. For a fast, you ate nothing. You would feast to celebrate a religious holiday, or someone's birthday, or a famous battle, or a great victory over your enemies. You would fast for two reasons: either as punishment for something terrible that you had done or to show how religious you were.

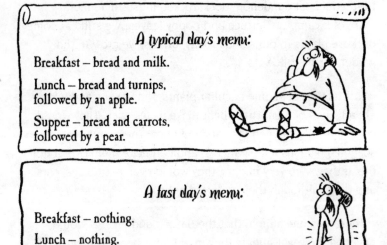

A typical day's menu:

Breakfast – bread and milk.

Lunch – bread and turnips, followed by an apple.

Supper – bread and carrots, followed by a pear.

A fast day's menu:

Breakfast – nothing.
Lunch – nothing.
Supper – nothing.

A feast day's menu:

Breakfast – bread and milk.

Lunch – bread and cabbage, followed by some blackberries.

Supper – the boiled tongue of an ox, the roast leg of a young lamb, a roasted duck and a roasted partridge, a bowl of rabbit stew, a salad of raw carrots, cabbages, nettles, lettuce and onions, followed by eggs with blackberries and strawberries, and a plate of figs and plums. All this would be accompanied by some French wine and some English beer. (Wine had to be imported from France or Germany, so it was reserved for special occasions.)

At a feast, there would be entertainment. A singer might play music on a harp or a lyre, and sing some songs. (Harps and lyres are stringed instrument that you play by plucking the strings.) A poet would stand up at the end of the table, and recite some verses. As well as poetry, music and singing, other entertainers would dance, joke, riddle and juggle.

Cooking the Books

Only the very rich would own books. Therefore, most people did not have cookery books. Recipes were passed down through the family. You learnt how to cook by watching other people cooking. The same applied to table manners. No one wrote down manuals of manners; they were simply passed from parent to child. If you visited a Saxon home, and ate with the family, you might be a bit disgusted by the way people ate.

People used their fingers to eat. The Saxons and Vikings used simple spoons and knives, but no other cutlery. Forks had not been invented yet. Instead, everyone carried a knife all the time. You would use your knife in three different ways: hunting animals, protecting yourself if you were ever attacked, and cutting up your food at meals.

Everyone shared the same plates; you just picked at food on big plates, rather than transferring your food onto your own individual plate. In the same way, people would not use their own cups or glasses; water would be served in a big jug or goblet, and people would pass it around the room to whoever wanted a drink.

You might be thinking that this sounds extremely unhealthy. If one person had a disease, didn't everyone get it? The simple answer is yes. Saxon life was very unhealthy. You were lucky if you lived past the age of thirty. If you didn't catch a nasty disease from sharing a goblet with someone, you might be eaten by a bear, murdered by a Viking or get lost in the forest.

Savour the Flavour

If you ate nothing but bread and vegetables, your taste buds would get bored very quickly. So, the Saxons and Vikings tried to add interesting tastes to their foods. Unlike us, they didn't have factories or laboratories to experiment with unusual ingredients. They could only use whatever they could find in the forest.

They had no sugar, only honey. The bees were not kept in hives. They lived freely among the trees where they made their nests. Brave or foolish people would steal the honey from the bees, sometimes returning with delicious sweet honeycombs, at other times earning nothing more than some painful bee stings.

Some herbs could be found in London. You would simply have to wander into the local forest to pick up mint, mustard, parsley, chervil, coriander and poppies. Salt was also easy to find if you left some seawater in the hot summer sun, the water would evaporate, leaving salt behind. However, other spices had to be imported from foreign countries, so they were extremely expensive. Only the rich could afford to flavour their food with interesting spices like pepper, cinnamon or nutmeg.

CHAPTER FIVE

The First Voyage of Erik the Viking

Water slapped against the front of the longboat. Wind filled the large square sail. Thirty men huddled on the deck, wrapping their cloaks around their bodies to keep out the cold. They were frozen and hungry, but none of them complained. Their thoughts were focused on the day ahead, the battle that would be fought, and the treasure that might be won.

Of the thirty, the youngest was only thirteen years old. His name was Erik. This was the first year that he had been allowed to sail from the village and join the attacks on England. He felt nervous, but he knew that he must hide his fear. If he showed any sign of fear, he would be left behind before the battle, or even thrown into the sea and forced to swim. That would be his punishment for behaving like a boy rather than a man.

He crouched by the side of the boat, and peered at the horizon. There! He could see the thin line of land. That was England. The home of the Saxons. In a few hours, they would reach the shore, where they would meet the nine other boats that had sailed with them.

Erik glanced along the length of the boat. He knew every one of the thirty men aboard. All of them lived in the same village as him. Every year, in the spring, the men of the village climbed into their boats and set sail. Every autumn, they would return to the village, laden with treasure. For the past twelve years, Erik had watched the men leave in the spring, and waited for their return in the autumn. Now, for the first time, he was allowed to accompany them.

He reached under the thick lining of his cloak, and checked his weapons. A dagger was fastened to his belt. Slung over his back, he carried a small axe. Lying at his feet, he had his spear and his shield. Ever since he was a child, he had practised fighting with these weapons. Now, for the first time, he would have the chance to use them in anger. Rather than play-fighting with his father or his friends, he would have to defend himself against real blows, and attack with real strength. By the end of today, he might have killed his first Saxon.

The Boat

Every winter, the Vikings returned to the village and repaired their boats. Over the years, they had become expert seafarers. Erik was only thirteen years old, but he was already an experienced sailor. He could mend a sail, a rope or a broken board in the bottom of the boat. If the other sailors found themselves in trouble, he could even steer the boat and man the sails. During the day, he could plot his position in the ocean by using the sun; at night, he would use the stars.

All the Vikings sailed the same type of boat, built from oak trees, riveted together with metal for strength. They called it a longship. It was long and thin, with one big rectangular sail and a long row of oars on either side. In the middle of the ocean, they used the sail; in the river or when the wind died down, they used the oars. At the front of the ship, the Vikings carved a decoration – a dragon's head, for instance – to scare anyone who saw the ship coming.

The longships had an open deck and no cabin. In the rain and snow, the sailors got wet and cold. In a storm, water splashed over the deck. They slept in sleeping-bags made from animal skin, and ate bread which was soaked in seawater. Many Vikings died on the voyage, either from the wet and the cold, or drowning when the boat capsized, or being swept over the side by a big wave.

In their boats, the Vikings travelled to more places than just England. They went to the Shetland Islands and the Orkneys; they travelled east to Russia and south to Turkey; they sailed across the huge empty expanses of the Atlantic Ocean, starting settlements in Iceland, Greenland and even North America.

Why did they take these terrible risks? Why did they travel in such difficult conditions?

The Prize

As the longship sailed down the Thames, the men took their places, lifted the oars from their resting-places and slid them into the water. They started rowing. The wind filled the sails. The boat moved quickly through the water, heading towards London.

Erik was the youngest person on the boat, and he had no particular task. He was here to watch and learn. If any of the Vikings were killed or wounded, he would take their place. Until that happened, he stood at the back of the boat, behind the steersman, watching everything that happened. He turned round, and

42

glanced back down the river. He could see eight more longships. Each of them held thirty Vikings. Together, they formed a real army.

On the bank of the river, Erik saw a shepherd, surrounded by a flock of sheep. The shepherd stared in amazement at the boats. Then he turned around, and started running towards the thick forests.

Erik tugged the sleeve of the man standing nearest to him, and said, 'Won't he warn the others that we're coming?'

'We're quicker than him,' replied the man. 'By the time he gets to the city, we'll have landed already.'

The river curled around a big bend, then another, and Erik got his first sight of London. It was the biggest place that he had ever seen. At home, his village had thirty or forty houses. London had several hundred. He stared at the town in amazement and fear, wondering what would happen next.

As the boat came towards the shore, four men hurried to the mast and pulled down the sail. Four more jumped overboard, carrying thick ropes, and ran onto the pebbly beach. They pulled the boat onto the shore, and tied the ropes around a nearby tree. Along the beach, the other boats were landing. The Vikings leaped over the sides of the boats, grabbed their weapons, and hurried towards London. Erik held his spear in one hand, his shield in the other, and ran with them.

The attack was a complete surprise. The foolish natives had made no preparations. Some were eating. Others were sleeping. Many more must have wandered into the forest to collect food or shepherd their animals. As Erik ran around the town, following the other Vikings, he saw scenes of blood, slaughter and death – but it was always the Saxons who died, and never the Vikings. The stupid Saxons didn't have a chance. The clever ones ran away as fast as they could. The stupid ones tried to fight, using whatever they could grab – a dagger, a wooden spoon, a pot from the fire. Their weapons were useless against the sharp swords and spears wielded by the Vikings.

Crowds of Vikings charged into the houses, and stole whatever they could carry. If any of the Saxons tried to resist, the Vikings killed them. Men, women, children, dogs, cats – the Vikings didn't care who they killed. It was all part of the fun of being a Viking.

That day, Erik did not kill anyone. He was too young and too weak. He watched the others, and learnt from them. However, he did do some proper Viking work: he carried armfuls of loot from the houses to the ships. He led two sheep and a goat to the boat, and loaded a sack with jewellery, silk, cheese, ham and daggers. When they had finished raiding the town, their longship was laden with treasure, and so heavy that Erik worried whether they could get home without sinking.

His worries were unfounded. They sailed safely home with all their treasure. The next year, Erik sailed again to England, and killed his first Saxon. He was fourteen years old. After that, he sailed to England every year, killed a few Saxons, and stole lots of treasure.

'This is the life,' Erik used to say, as the longship plunged through the waves towards London. 'The life of the Viking.'

How Viking Are You?

Have you got what it takes to be a Viking?

Take this simple test to see how Viking YOU are.

QUESTION ONE
Do you like killing people?

(a) Yes, I don't feel happy unless I kill at least one person every week.

(b) No, I think killing people is wrong.

QUESTION TWO
Do you like pretty flowers?

(a) Yes, I like stamping on pretty flowers and mushing them up.

(b) Yes, I like picking pretty flowers and putting them in a pretty vase.

QUESTION THREE
Do you like boats?

(a) Yes, I love boats.

(b) No, I get seasick if I even see a picture of a boat.

QUESTION FOUR

If you saw a woman wearing a beautiful gold necklace, would you...

(a) Steal it.

(b) Tell the woman how beautiful she looked.

QUESTION FIVE

Which is your favourite weapon, an axe or a spear?

(a) I like an axe for chopping people up and a spear for throwing at people.

(b) I already told you, I think killing people is wrong.

Answers: If you answered (a) to all the questions, then you'd probably make a great Viking. If you answered (b) to all the questions, then you should run as fast as you can if you ever see a Viking coming towards you.

CHAPTER SIX

Attacking and Defending London

The battles between the Vikings and the Saxons weren't always so simple. When he was older, Erik had to fight some real battles, where Vikings died as well as Saxons. For three hundred years, the Vikings and the Saxons fought over London. During that time, they got to know one another very well.

Because the Saxons and the Vikings spent so many years fighting one another, they used more or less the same weapons. If any of them developed a new weapon, the others would find out about it extremely quickly, and copy the design.

When the Saxons and the Vikings fought one another, they had three main varieties of weaponry: throwing weapons, hand weapons and weapons used for protection.

Throwing Weapons

Before the real battle began, the two armies threw missiles at one another, hoping to scare the enemy and knock out a few of his troops.

The simplest type of throwing weapon was a javelin – a stick with a sharp point. A Saxon javelin looked just like the javelins used by modern athletes.

A longbow was more complex to design, build and use. To make a bow, you take a long, bendy piece of wood and tie a cord between the two ends. A longbow has two big advantages over a javelin: firstly, it is much more accurate; secondly, you don't actually have to throw it at your enemy. If you carry a stock of spare arrows, you can use the bow over and over again.

The Saxons also used small axes, which they threw through the air, and slings, which they used to hurl small stones at the enemy. A sling is a very simple weapon: you put a rock in a piece of cloth, twirl it round and round your head, and let go. The rock shoots through the air. If you have a good aim, it hits the enemy's head. Even if it doesn't kill him, it will give him a horrible headache, so he won't fight so well.

There is one obvious problem with throwing a missile at your enemy: he can pick it up and throw it right back again. This might continue for hours: the two armies would throw the same javelins back and forth, back and forth, until they got bored. Then, they would do some real fighting.

Hand Weapons

The Saxons and Vikings had two main weapons for hand-to-hand fighting: the sword and the spear.

The spear was the most common weapon. It had a sharp iron head and wooden shaft, usually cut from an ash tree, although other wood might be used, such as hazel, apple, oak and maple. The shaft would be about the same length as a man's height. Shorter spears would be thrown, and the longer ones were used in hand-to-hand combat.

A sword would be two-edged. Both sides of the blade were sharpened, so you could cut back and forth, chopping your enemy with both swings. The blade would be decorated. If the sword had a name (and many of them did) it would be written on the blade. Every sword owner used a scabbard to protect him from his own blade – otherwise he would cut himself – and to protect the blade from bashing against things.

Poor men used spears and rich men used swords. Because metal was so expensive, a good sword would be passed from father to son, and used by many different men over the years. The best swords would live longer than many men – and kill many men too. However, some warriors preferred to be buried with their sword: when a great warrior was placed in his grave, his sword would be placed in his cold, stiff hands, so he would be fully prepared if he ever came back to life.

Protect and Survive

The best places to attack someone with your sword were his head, his sword arm or his legs. In a battle, the rest of his body would have been protected by his shield or his mail.

The Saxons and Vikings used round shields made from wood, with a metal rim and centre. Sometimes, their shields were painted bright colours to scare the enemy. People used both small and large shields. You could choose whichever you wanted. Small shields are lighter, so you can move around more easily, but large shields offer more protection. If you lost your sword or spear, you could use the shield as a weapon, and beat your enemy with it.

In a battle, men would stand together in a line, because a line of shields was impossible to break through. It was called a shieldwall. If your army managed to break the shieldwall, you were half-way to victory.

The most important men in the army wore mail. This doesn't mean that they were covered in letters. Mail was a long shirt made from metal, which offered good protection against a sword or a spear.

Going Berserk!

In a battle, it's very important to make your enemy feel afraid. Then, he is more likely to turn around and run away.

That's where the word 'berserk' comes from. The berserkers were warriors who worked themselves into a frenzy before battle. Like mad dogs, they yelled and howled, frothed at the mouth, yapped, bit people, and looked like complete loonies. Sometimes, they went into battle wearing no clothes, naked apart from a sword and a spear.

If you saw a huge naked man running towards you, screaming at the top of his voice and waving his sword above his head, wouldn't you feel frightened? Would you stand and fight? Or would you be tempted to turn round and run away?

CHAPTER SEVEN

King Alfred the Great

Every year, the Vikings clambered into their boats, sailed across the North Sea to England and attacked the Saxons. It got pretty boring for everyone. Whenever the Saxons had gathered some good crops, reared a healthy brood of chickens or saved some money, the Vikings sailed to England and took whatever they wanted for themselves.

After some time, the Saxons felt fed up. But there wasn't much they could do. They had tried asking the Vikings to stop, but the Vikings just laughed. They had tried fighting the Vikings, but the Vikings were bigger and stronger, and had no difficulty chopping them in little pieces. They tried running away, but the Vikings could always run faster.

In AD 835, the Vikings attacked the Isle of Sheppey, an island on the River Thames. From then on, their attacks became more daring and more dangerous. They ventured further and further up the Thames. In AD 851, they mounted a huge raid on London. They killed many people, stole a huge amount of gold and goods, and left a trail of burning houses. But there was vital change during that raid: rather than going home to Scandinavia, the Vikings stayed in England.

Usually, the Vikings sailed into a place, stole what they could, killed who they could, and sailed away again. This time, they stayed. The Vikings didn't want to come to London just for their summer holidays. Now, they wanted to live here.

By the year AD 871, all of England had been conquered by the Vikings except the kingdom of Wessex. In that year, the Vikings launched a triumphant attack on Wessex. The King of Wessex, Ethelred, died. The Vikings were sure that they had managed to conquer the whole country. From now on, they thought, they would have the country to themselves.

However, they had not expected the courage and determination of the new king of Wessex. His name was Alfred, and he devoted himself to fighting the Vikings. Only one British king is remember as 'the Great.' Other kings and queens have been good and bad, stupid and clever, boring and interesting, successes and failures, bald and hairy, but only one of them has been great.

Essex, Wessex, Sussex – Where's Norsex?

You probably know the names Sussex and Essex. They are counties near London which still exist. A thousand years ago, they were the Kingdom of the East Saxons and the Kingdom of the South Saxons. Over the years, the names changed, adapting into Essex and Sussex.

The West Saxons had a kingdom too, which was called Wessex. That doesn't exist any more, but you can still find references to Wessex in old books. A famous writer called Thomas Hardy wrote a whole series of novels set in Wessex. You might have heard of the most famous ones, *Tess of the D'Urbevilles* and *Far From the Madding Crowd*.

And what about Norsex? What happened to the Kingdom of the North Saxons? The Saxons who lived in the north got thoroughly trampled by the Vikings, who took over all the territory in that part of England. Norsex never existed.

Alfred: Great King, Terrible Cook

King Elthelwulf, the King of Wessex, had four sons. Their names were Ethelbad, Ethlebert, Ethelred and Alfred. (You might be wondering why Alfred got a normal name, and his three elder brothers got such silly names. I was wondering that too. Alfred's parents are the only people who could answer that question, and they've been dead for more than a thousand years.) While Alfred was growing up, the Vikings

attacked England more and more often. King Elthelwulf thought that God was punishing him. He didn't know what he had done wrong – but he knew that he must have done something terrible, otherwise God wouldn't be punishing him so cruelly. He decided to send his youngest son to Rome where he could talk to the Pope and ask why God was so angry. Ethelwulf couldn't go to Rome himself because he was so busy fighting the Vikings.

Alfred travelled all the way from London to Rome, and asked the Pope why God was so angry. The Pope didn't know. After Rome, Alfred travelled to France, where he met King Charles the Bald. At the time, Alfred was only five years old, so he probably didn't say much to the Pope or King Charles.

Over the next twenty years, when Alfred returned from his European travels, he learnt how to fight. He hunted wild animals and fought the Vikings. When King Elthelwulf died, the Saxons decided that his youngest son would make the best king. They gave the crown to Alfred.

At first, Alfred was not successful. The Vikings took over more and more of the country, forcing Alfred and his men to take shelter in the swamps of Althenay in Somerset. There are several legends about Alfred's time in the swamps. One of the legends says that Alfred dressed as a musician and sneaked into the Viking camp; there, he played beautiful music and managed to overhear the battle plans that the Vikings were plotting.

Another legend says that Alfred took shelter in a village. His hostess asked him to watch some cakes that she was cooking, and make sure that they didn't burn. Alfred was thinking about his plans for defeating the Vikings, and completely forgot the cakes. They burnt to a crisp. The woman returned and shouted at him. 'Look! You complete idiot! You've burnt my cakes!'

'I'm sorry,' said Alfred. 'I'm terribly sorry.'

'Sorry isn't good enough,' shouted the woman. 'That's not going to bring back my cakes, is it?'

Of course, she didn't realise that she was talking to the king.

Whether or not he really burnt the cakes, Alfred organised his men into a strong army, fought the Vikings and defeated them. He drove them out of Wessex. Five years later, he led his army through England, arrived at London, and drove the Vikings out of the city. At that point, the Vikings surrendered and made an agreement with Alfred. They divided England two separate kingdoms, the north and the south. The Vikings ruled the north while Alfred ruled the south.

If Alfred hadn't fought that battle, or if he had lost to the Vikings, the history of England would have been completely different. The Vikings would have conquered the whole country. They would have ruled London. Today, we wouldn't speak English – we would speak Danish. We wouldn't drink tea and eat toast and Jaffa Cakes – we would drink very, very strong coffee and eat Danish pastries and frikadellers. London would be one small part of the Viking Empire.

Compared to Copenhagen, the Danish capital, London might just be a little town where nothing much happened. If you're glad that Londoners speak English rather than Norwegian or Danish, you should thank King Alfred.

Alfred or Arthur?

King Arthur was the most famous British king of Saxon times. There are many wonderful legends about him and his court. Everyone knows about Sir Lancelot, Guinevere and the Sword in the Stone. However, there is no actual evidence that King Arthur ever existed. Perhaps he was invented by the British when they needed a great hero to inspire their battles. Or perhaps a storyteller started telling stories about him, and everyone thought the stories were so exciting that they must be true. For whatever reason, King Arthur has become a figure that everyone recognises, a name that everyone knows – although he might never have lived.

Sounds Souper

Modern English is a mixture of lots of different languages. Over the centuries, many different people from many different places have lived in England, and each of them have added their own words and phrases to the language.

You could imagine the English language as a soup.

Different people have added different ingredients to the soup. The Romans put some solid grammar at the bottom of the soup; that's the meat which gives the soup its flavour. The Angles and Saxons added some good solid vegetables: leeks, carrots, swedes and turnips. The Vikings threw in a few strange Scandinavian ingredients: the hoof of an ox, the horn of a bull. When the Normans arrived, they added some interesting French ingredients: a handful of snails, some steak, a couple of endives. Over the years since then, other people have added a whole variety of different spices and flavourings until the language tasted as it does now. A rich, strongly flavoured soup.

But the soup isn't finished yet. People continue adding ingredients to it. Every day, all around the world, people add words to the English soup, changing the grammar and the vocabulary, making the soup taste even more delicious. With all the different ingredients which are added every day, the language becomes even more interesting to speak and write.

The Saxons wrote and spoke in a very different way to us. It's extremely difficult for us to understand their language. The Saxon alphabet was completely different to ours. We can't read it – just as Saxons wouldn't be able to read any of our books. However, just like us the Saxons loved stories and poems.

The most famous Saxon poem is called 'Beowulf'. Beowulf is the name of a king, who fights a vicious monster called Grendel. He kills the monster. Then, years later, when Beowulf is an old man, he fights a fire-breathing dragon. He wins the fight, but the dragon wounds him, and he dies. The poem ends with his funeral. Happy stuff, eh?

The poem is still with us today. If you want to read a translation of this poem, you should be able to find it in your local library or bookshop. There is only one copy of the original 'Beowulf' left in the entire world. It's very fragile, so don't ask to touch the manuscript but you can see it in the British Library, near King's Cross Station.

CHAPTER EIGHT

Lundenburh

In the year AD 900, Alfred died. He was fifty-one years old. However, his influence continued in England, because he had made so many important changes to the country during his reign. He also made many important changes to London, the biggest of which was persuading Londoners to live in a new part of the city.

When Alfred was thirty-eight years old, he learnt to read and write. He decided that reading and writing were great. He made a law saying that all noblemen should learn to read and write, and ordered one of his bishops to start writing down a history of England. One day, Alfred hoped, all English men would be able to read and write.

This wasn't his only idea for improving his kingdom. Alfred was a visionary leader who had many new ideas about how to organise a country, and much of his success stemmed from his organisational skill. He created the first English navy. He divided the army into two halves, ordering one half of the men to stay at home while the other half did military duty. Then they swapped. Like that, there were always some soldiers ready to fight and some farmers working in the fields. He forced the farmers who weren't fighting to send two men to the army for every plough that they owned. Alternatively, they could choose to pay a fine – and the army would use the money to hire more soldiers.

He also ordered the English citizens to protect themselves by fortifying their towns with strong walls. Alfred knew that the Vikings would continue attacking the country and, if the towns weren't protected, the Vikings would conquer them.

The Empty City

As you will remember, the Roman part of London remained unoccupied for several hundred years after the Romans left Britain. The Saxons chose not to live within the Roman walls, preferring to build their villages elsewhere.

This all changed when Alfred became King of the Saxons. He saw that the Romans had known how to build fortifications – big stone walls – which were tall and strong enough to protect the citizens from attackers. Alfred persuaded Londoners to move into the old Roman walls. In other words, they moved from Lundenwic to Lundenburh, from modern Covent Garden to modern

St Paul's. In the Saxon dialect, the word 'burh' means 'a fortified town.' So, Lundenburh was the Saxon city inside the old Roman walls.

Alfred had a plan for England: he wanted the country to be covered with fortified towns – burhs – where the population could protect themselves when the Vikings attacked. He said that there should be a burh every thirty miles throughout the country. Wherever you were, you would never be more than fifteen miles from a burh. If you heard that the Vikings were coming, you could jump on a horse or start running, and try to get inside a burh before the Vikings arrived.

London Bridge Has Fallen Down

Lundenburh was beside the site of London Bridge. No-one knows when the first bridge was built, nor how long it lasted. There is a legend that the Saxons built London Bridge, but the Vikings pulled it down when they invaded the city. The legend says that the Vikings tied ropes to the bridge, then sailed towards the sea, pulling the bridge into the river. That, people say, is where the song comes from. (London Bridge is falling down, falling down, London Bridge is falling... oh, you know the rest.) The Vikings had an even earlier version of the song – a poem written by their poet, Ottar Svarte, which went like this:

London bridge has fallen down.
We've won the gold and the crown.
The clash of shields!
The blast of trumpets!
With Odin's help, we smash their heads,
and our arrows knock them dead.

From historical evidence, we only know one thing about London Bridge in Saxon times: witches were thrown off it to punish them for practising black magic. In the tenth century, according to a book written at the time, a woman was found guilty of witchcraft. The woman made a small statue out of wax. The statue represented a nobleman who had mistreated her. Whenever she wanted to take revenge on him, she stuck a pin in the statue, and the nobleman would suffer horrible agony. He would feel terrible pains in his body – in exactly the same places as the pins in the statues. When the woman was caught, she was arrested, tied up with rope, and thrown off London Bridge.

Lord of the Runes

If you look at a picture of a Saxon sword, you might see some strange lettering along the blade. These strange letters are called runes. They were the Saxon alphabet.

The Saxon alphabet was slightly different from our modern alphabet. They had some letters that we don't use, and we use some letters that they didn't have. When archaeologists dig up Saxon villages or tombs, they have found coins, swords, plates, brooches and all kinds of other objects covered with runes.

Here is the alphabet of Saxon runes:

Why not try writing your name in runes?

King Canute

Swein Forkbeard, the King of
Denmark, sailed across the sea
with a big army, and invaded
England. Among his army, he
bought his son, a young man
named Canute. Thirty years later,
Canute was not only the king of
England, but of Denmark,
Sweden and Norway too. He
ruled all four countries at the
same time.

He was a brutal man: if
anyone disobeyed him, he cut
off their nose. If he was really
angry, he cut off their hands too. If he was absolutely furious,
he would chop off their feet. If you saw someone with no
hands, feet or nose, you knew that they must have really
irritated Canute. As you can imagine, people were very careful
not to annoy him.

King Canute was so successful that he started to believe he
could do anything and rule everything – even the sea. 'I shall
command the sea not to come in,' he told his courtiers. 'What
do you think of that? Is it a good idea?'

'That's an excellent idea, your majesty,' said the courtiers.
They were frightened of him, and didn't dare disagree with him.

Together, Canute and his courtiers went down to the sea. It was low tide. A long expanse of wet sand stretched to the waves. Canute instructed his courtiers to place his throne beside the sea. He sat in his throne, put his gold crown on his head, and pointed at the sea. 'Listen to me,' he shouted in his deep royal voice. 'I, King Canute, King of the English, the Danish, the Swedish and the Norwegians, make this demand of you, the sea. I order you to stay where you are. Today, the tide will not rise. Today, the sea will stay in its place. That is the will of King Canute, and my will shall be obeyed.'

The waves swooshed across the water, but the sea didn't answer.

An hour later, the tide had risen. Water lapped around Canute's feet. He sat in his throne and pointed at the sea. 'No further, sea! Come no further! That is the commandment of King Canute.'

But the sea kept coming. The waves came up to Canute's ankles... then up to his knees... then up to his waist. Canute stayed sitting on his throne, and shouted at the sea once more. 'No further, sea! Come no further! That is the commandment of King Canute.'

The sea kept rising, covering Canute's waist, then his belly, and all the way up to his shoulders. Finally, a big wave splashed over Canute's head, and washed off his crown. His courtiers ran forward and grabbed Canute – but his crown was gone forever, swept out on the waves, swallowed by the sea.

Although this story makes Canute sound like an idiot, he was actually a clever man. (The story, as you might have guessed, probably isn't true.) He ruled a huge empire. However, like many powerful rulers, he didn't think very hard about who would rule when he was dead. His wife was a Frenchwoman called Emma. She was from Normandy – which gave William the Norman an excuse to come and conquer England later in the century.

Although London was Canute's capital, he didn't like the city. He preferred Winchester. No one knows why he didn't like London. The terrible traffic? All the cars and lorries jamming up the streets? The pollution? All those sticky journeys on the tube? No – he couldn't have hated them because none of them had been invented yet. For whatever reason, Canute disliked London and, when he died, he chose to be buried in Winchester.

Funny Names

If you were an important Viking or Saxon, you needed a funny name. That was how people knew how important you were.

Here are some names from Viking and Saxon times. I have invented four of them, but the others belonged to famous people. Can you guess which ones are invented and which are real?

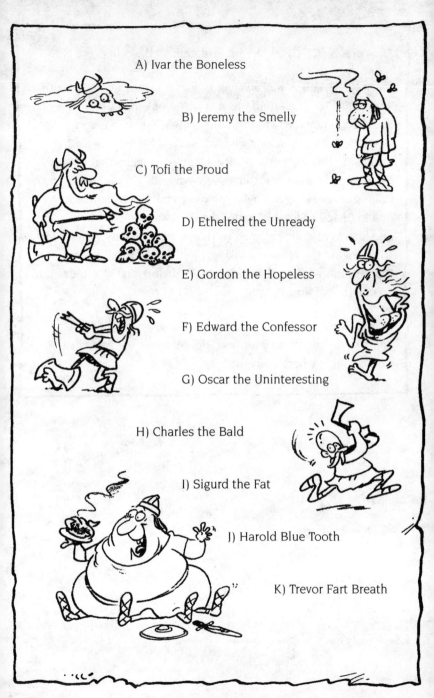

A) Ivar the Boneless

B) Jeremy the Smelly

C) Tofi the Proud

D) Ethelred the Unready

E) Gordon the Hopeless

F) Edward the Confessor

G) Oscar the Uninteresting

H) Charles the Bald

I) Sigurd the Fat

J) Harold Blue Tooth

K) Trevor Fart Breath

Answers: B), C), G) and K) are invented; all the others are real!

Ivar the Boneless was a Viking king who invaded England with a big army. Tofi the Proud was a Danish nobleman who lived and died in London, where he was buried. Ethelred the Unready was a Saxon king who lost several battles against the Vikings. The name 'unready' doesn't actually mean that he was never ready in time; it means 'badly-advised.' Edward the Confessor was King of England – you can discover more about him in Chapter Eleven. Charles the Bald was King of France, and he was roundly defeated by the Vikings when they attacked Paris. Sigurd the Fat was a Viking, the Earl of Orkney. Harold Blue Tooth was the father of Swein Forkbeard, and also the grandfather of King Canute.

If you were an important Saxon or Viking, what would your name be? What would your best friend's name be? And what would your teacher's name be?

CHAPTER TEN

Religion

London has always been home to lots of different religions. At different times in history, different rulers have decided that their religion is the only correct religion, and all the other religions are wrong. If anyone else tries to continue with a different religion, they usually get burnt, hanged, drowned or dropped in a big cauldron of boiling oil.

During the time that the Saxons and Vikings lived in London, there was a huge shift from one religion to another. The Saxons and the Vikings were pagans. They believed in lots of different gods rather than just one god. They believed that each god looked after a different part of life. If you were going to war, you prayed to one god – the god of war. If you wanted your crops to grow well, you prayed to another god – the god of good crops. If you wanted to have a child, you prayed to yet another god – the god of children. This all got pretty confusing, which might be why the Saxons liked Christianity so much. If you're a Christian, you just pray to one God, and he takes care of everything.

How did Christianity come to London? Like this...

One hot afternoon, a man named Gregory was walking through the market in Rome. He was a priest. He looked at all the different things for sale in the market: flowers, apples, cabbages, candles, interesting stones, walking sticks, goats, slaveboys.

Gregory didn't need a slave boy. He lived in a monastery, where all the work was done by the monks. However, he stopped and stared at two of the slave boys. They were young and thin. Their blonde hair and pale skin looked very unusual in the Roman market, where almost everyone was dark, swarthy and tanned by the hot Italian sun. Gregory walked over to the slave trader, pointed at the boys and asked, 'Who are these two angels?'

The slave trader replied, 'They are not angels but Angles.'

'Angles?' said Gregory.

'Yes, Angles.'

'What does that mean? What are Angles?'

'They are people from Angle-Land,' explained the slave trader.

'And where is Angle-Land?'

'Oh, it's a long way away,' said the slave trader. 'A cold and miserable place. Rains all day. The sun never shines.' He turned to the two slave boys, and grinned at them. 'You're much happier here, aren't you?' He pinched one of the slave boy's cheeks. Neither of the slave boys said anything. They didn't look too happy. Probably, they had been beaten earlier in the day; that was what usually happened to slave boys. Then the slave trader turned back to Gregory. 'I can give you a good price if you're interested.'

'No, thank you,' said Gregory.

'They're excellent slaves,' said the slave trader. 'Each of them comes with a full certificate of health and a two-year guarantee. Tell you what, it's been a slow day. You can have two Angles for the price of one.'

Gregory shook his head, and walked away. Later that afternoon, the two slave boys were sold to a rich widow whose cook had just died of malaria. Gregory never saw them again. However, he never forgot them.

Thirty years later...

A serious-minded young man called Augustine was sitting in the library in Rome, reading the Bible, when one of the monks came to fetch him. 'Quick,' whispered the monk. 'Come with me.'

Augustine didn't like being disturbed when he was reading. 'I'll come later,' he said in a grumpy voice. 'I'm busy now.'

'Later won't do,' said the monk. 'Pope Gregory wants to see you now.'

Augustine's eyes widened. He put down the book, stood up, and followed the monk out of the library. When the Pope wants to see you, it is considered extremely bad manners to keep him waiting.

It was a great honour to meet the Pope, and Augustine wondered why he had been summoned. Was the Pope going to reward him? Or promote him? Perhaps the Pope would ask him to become a bishop! A bishop, thought Augustine. I'd love to be a bishop. He started imagining how he would look, dressed in a bishop's robes, with a big bishop's hat on his head.

When Augustine reached the Pope's rooms, he had already planned how he would re-decorate the nice big house that bishops were always given. However, he quickly realised that he wasn't going to be made a bishop. Pope Gregory sat him down, offered him a glass of water, and said, 'I want you to do something for me, Augustine. I want you to leave Rome and travel to a foreign country. When you get there, you must spread the gospel, and convert the population to Christianity. Will you be able to do that?'

'I think so,' said Augustine. 'I hope so. But I have one question, Your Holiness. Where is this country?'

'It is the country of the Angles,' replied Gregory.

'The Angles? Don't you mean the Angels?'

'No, no, I mean the Angles,' said Gregory. (As you might have guessed already, Pope Gregory was the same man who had walked through the slave market, thirty years earlier.) He said, 'I have heard it called Angle-Land, or even England. So, will you be ready to leave tomorrow?'

79

The following morning at dawn, Augustine left Rome with a few monks whom he had carefully chosen for their courage and intelligence. The journey from Rome to London was long and difficult. As they travelled north, the air grew colder. The natives were unfriendly. After a few days, Augustine sent a letter back to Gregory, suggesting that the mission was a mistake, and asking permission to turn round and return to Rome. Gregory's reply was simple: keep going, he said, and do what I asked you to do.

Augustine arrived in England. He saw immediately that England was a cold, miserable country. The clouds never left the sky. Rain poured down constantly. The local population never washed their clothes, and smelt terrible. The food was awful. Augustine wanted one thing and one thing only: to go back to Rome. But he knew that there was no point arguing with Pope Gregory. He started preaching to the smelly Saxons, telling them the story of the Bible. At first, the Saxons just laughed at him. Then, one by one, they started listening. And when they listened, they discovered that they liked what they were hearing. Within a year, Augustine had converted ten thousand people to Christianity.

Augustine was so successful, he decided to built a big church at Canterbury, which became the most important church in England. Augustine became the first Archbishop of Canterbury. He also appointed two other bishops in England, one in Rochester and the other in London.

St Paul's

About twenty years after Augustine brought Christianity to England, the Bishop of London decided to build a cathedral. His name was Bishop Mellitus. He built a large church – the largest in England at that time – and called it after one of the greatest of the Christian saints, St Paul. That was one thousand and four hundred years ago. Ever since, a cathedral has stood in that place, bearing that name.

Viking Religion

The Vikings had their own religion. They worshipped interesting gods who led wild and crazy lives. Here are some of them:

Odin was the boss of the gods, also known as the All-Father. To drink from the spring of wisdom, he gave up one of his eyes. He was the god of battle. Odin lived in a Great Hall called Valhalla, where some humans would go after their deaths, if they had shown particular courage in the way that they died. If you died gloriously in battle, for instance, you would get the chance to spend all eternity having fun with Odin in Valhalla, fighting all day and feasting all night.

Freyja was the wife of Odin. She was the goddess of love. However, being a Viking god, she liked war too. She rode into battle in a chariot drawn by two cats.

Thor was the god of wind and storm. (In fact, the word 'thunder' comes from his name – and the Vikings thought that thunder came from the noise of his chariot's wheels.) Thor was strong and straightforward. He carried a big hammer, and controlled the weather.

As you will have noticed, these are very similar to the gods worshipped by the Saxons. Although the Vikings and the Saxons spent a lot of time and energy fighting one another, they were actually very similar in their beliefs, their attitudes and the way that they lived.

The Vikings didn't like the idea of having just one god. They liked having lots of gods. They didn't understand why Jesus Christ couldn't take his place alongside Odin, Loki, Thor and all the other Viking gods. However, slowly the Vikings changed their minds. They decided that Christianity didn't sound like such a bad idea after all. Around about the same time that the Normans arrived in Britain, the Vikings accepted Christianity and rejected their old gods.

Days of the Week

You can still hear traces of the Viking gods in our daily life. Some of the days of the week are named after Viking gods. Can you guess which ones have been named after Tiw, Odin (also known as Woden), Thor and Freyja?

(In case you're interested, this is how the other days of the week got their names: Sunday is the day of the sun. Monday is the day of the Moon. Saturday is named after the Roman god, Saturn.)

Eostre Eggs

The Saxon goddess of the spring and the dawn was called Eostre.

In the beginning of the spring – usually around the end of March or the beginning of April – the Saxons would hold a big feast in her honour. The Saxons associated two things with Eostre: eggs and rabbits. The goddess would ride on a large rabbit, and she would bring lots of eggs.

Does this sound familiar? Eostre bunnies? Eostre eggs? And the word Eostre itself?

That's because Easter is a Saxon festival which was taken over by Christians. Next time you eat an Easter egg, remember that you're actually taking part in a Pagan festival which the Saxons would have celebrated too.

CHAPTER ELEVEN

The Normans

EDWARD the CONFESSOR

In 1042 a man called Edward the Confessor was the King of England. He got his nickname because he was so religious. Before Edward became King of England, he spent thirty years in France. When he returned, he decided to build a huge church in London. Although that actual church no longer exists, there is still a church on the same site.

He chose a place called Thorney Island. A church had existed there since about AD 500, built by King Ethelred. That was just a small, ordinary church. Edward wanted to build the biggest church in England – and he did. It was called Westminster Abbey.

The church was finished by the end of 1065. However, Edward was too ill to visit. On Christmas Day, he made his final public appearance, but the effort was too exhausting, and dealt a final blow to his frail body. He struggled back to his bed, and died. At the beginning of January 1066, his body was taken to the new church at Westminster, and buried under the altar.

Westminster Abbey still exists. Although the modern cathedral is a completely different building, it stands in the same place as Edward's church, so his corpse is still buried under the altar. Thorney Island is no longer an island. Where the river used to flow, only cars flow now.

Who Will Be King?

Edward had been married, but he and his wife Edith had no children. When he died, four different men claimed the English crown.

The youngest had the strongest claim: he was Edgar, Edward's nephew. However, he was too young to rule the kingdom with any success. That left three other candidates:

CANDIDATE NUMBER ONE
Harold, Earl of Wessex

He was named by Edward as the future king of England and had the support of the English. He was the brother of Edward's wife, Edith, so he had a strong claim to the crown. At the beginning of 1066, he was crowned king in Westminster Abbey. But that didn't prevent the other two men from pursuing their claims on the English crown.

CANDIDATE NUMBER TWO
William, son of the Duke of Normandy

He claimed that Edward had named him as the future king of England. Since Edward was dead, no one knew if this was true or not. Although the English nobles did not want to be ruled by William, the Pope declared the crown should go to him.

CANDIDATE NUMBER THREE
Harald Hardrada, the King of Norway.

No one supported him. However, he had a big army, and that made people listen to him. He sailed from Norway with three hundred ships, landed in Northern England, and quickly captured York.

If you were an ordinary Saxon, which of these three men would you choose as your king? Candidate One, the Saxon? Candidate Two, the Norman? Or Candidate Three, the Norwegian? And why?

If I had been a Saxon, I would have chosen Harold, Earl of Wessex, because he was also a Saxon. You wouldn't want to be ruled by the French or the Norwegians. Apart from anything else, you wouldn't have been able to understand a word they said.

In the end, the Saxons didn't have much choice about their king. The matter was decided by war. In 1066, two huge battles rocked England. First Harold, Earl of Wessex, marched north and defeated the army of Harold Hardrada. Then, Harold marched down to the South Coast and fought his second battle in ten days, this time against the French. His troops were tired, and they lost. Harold was killed. William won the prize: the English crown.

Call That a Cartoon?

The Bayeux tapestry is a Norman cartoon. Unlike modern cartoons, it wasn't printed on cheap paper and sold in every newsagent round the country. There is only one copy of the Bayeux tapestry, which was woven out of wool on a strip of linen, two hundred and thirty feet long.

It tells the story of the Norman Conquest. The tapestry was ordered and paid for by a man named Odo. He was the bishop of Bayeux, and brother of William the Conqueror. As you can imagine, the story told by the tapestry is extremely biased, because the tapestry was made by the Normans. It describes the Normans as strong, intelligent, brave warriors, and the Saxons as dithering ninnies who can't tell one end of a spear from the other.

William the Conqueror of London

William had defeated the English armies and invaded England. However, he had not yet conquered London.

He had a big, strong army. He could have marched straight to London, attacked the city, and conquered it. However, he chose not to.

Why not? For one simple reason: he wanted the people of London to invite him into their city. He didn't want to make an enemy of them. He knew that Londoners don't care too much who is their ruler, as long as he or she rules them well.

So, William approached London very slowly. He went to Dover, where he said this to the people: 'I will treat you in the same way that you treat me.' In other words, if the people fought viciously and violently, he would fight back viciously and violently. But if the people behaved peacefully, William would treat them peacefully. And that is exactly what happened.

When Dover had surrendered to William, he marched his army to Canterbury, then Winchester. Doing a big circle around London, he crossed the Thames and marched to Berkhampstead. There, he sent a message to London: 'Will you accept me as your king?'

The people of London thought about his message. They discussed it amongst themselves. Finally, they sent a message back to William. 'Okay, you can be our king.'

When William received this message from the people of London, he marched with his army to the city. In Westminster Abbey, he was crowned king on Christmas Day 1066.

Saxon and Viking London were finished. From that day onwards, London, like England, was ruled by the Normans.

But London has always been bigger, stronger and more important than any king, queen, prime minister or mayor. A ruler might be strong today, but tomorrow he will have lost his hair, his power and his life. Rulers die, but London lives forever…

PLACES TO VISIT

You will not be surprised to learn that there are very few Saxon places to visit in London. The Saxons lived in London more than a thousand years ago. Their homes were mostly built from wood and straw. They were lucky if their walls survived for the winter – and if they did, they would probably be burned down by the Vikings in the spring.

Only churches and city walls were built from stone. In London, a few of the city walls have survived – you can see some of them if you go to the Museum of London, for instance. There are some Anglo-Saxon churches in London, but they have been re-built so many times over the past thousand years that it's difficult to tell what is what. If you want to see Anglo-Saxon buildings, you might have to leave London and travel to Winchester (King Alfred's capital city) or Lindisfarne (a large, important monastery on an island off Northumbria).

However, there are a few good places to visit in London where you can see some remnants of the Saxons and the Vikings. Most of these are museums, where you can see pots, swords, jewellery and other interesting bits and pieces.

If you want to see even more Anglo-Saxon items in museums, you should go to Stockholm, Oslo or Copenhagen. When the Vikings came to London, they stole lots of valuables and took them back home to Sweden, Norway and Denmark, where they have stayed ever since.

The Museum of London, London Wall, EC2Y 5HN

This is a great museum full of interesting exhibits about the history of London. The section on Saxon and Viking London is only one small section of the museum, but the whole place is worth visiting. www.museumoflondon.org.uk. Tel 020 7600 3699.

The British Museum, Great Russell Street, Bloomsbury,

WC1B 3DG. Here you can see the extraordinary Anglo-Saxon objects retrieved from the excavations at Sutton Hoo in Suffolk. These aren't directly connected with London, but they show how wealthy Saxons would have lived and died. www.thebritishmuseum.ac.uk. Tel 020 7636 1555.

The British Library, 96 Euston Road, King's Cross, NW1 2DB

Along with almost every book ever published in the United Kingdom, the British Library has an amazing collection of Anglo-Saxon manuscripts, including the only original copy of Beowulf. These are sometimes on display and sometimes in storage; you should ring them first if there is something particular that you specially want to see. www.bl.uk. Tel 020 7412 7332.

Westminster Abbey, Westminster, SW1P 3PA

You can go into Westminster Abbey and see Edward the Confessor's tomb. The original building has completely disappeared, having been rebuilt many times since 1065, but Edward's tomb is still there. His bones are slowly rotting away inside a special tomb which is marked with these words:

'Edward the Confessor built the great Abbey church at this site. His body still rests here in this shrine which Henry III caused to be erected in 1268. And here, as FOUNDER OF WESTMINSTER ABBEY, his memory has ever been held in honour and grateful remembrance.'

Every year, a special service is held to remember Edward the Confessor; if you go to the Abbey on St Edward's Day (13 October) you can attend the service. www.westminster-abbey.org. Tel 020 7222 5152.

There are a few other churches in London which were built by the Saxons. However, they have been rebuilt so many times over the past thousand years that you can hardly distinguish what is Saxon and what isn't.

The best way to see Saxon London is this: stand somewhere in London and close your eyes. (Chose a safe place to do this: don't stand in the middle of the road or near any open windows.)

With your eyes shut, imagine that you can't hear the sounds of the modern city; instead, you can hear mooing cows and singing birds, the wind in the trees, the shouts of people working in the fields. Imagine that you can't smell the pollution of the modern city; instead, you can smell poo and roast meat. Imagine that you're surrounded by the forest. Imagine that you're wearing a loose smock, and a dagger is tucked in your belt. Under your bare feet, you can feel the earth. Imagine that you're breathing the clean, fresh air.

Now, open your eyes. What do you see?

OTHER BOOKS FROM WATLING STREET YOU'LL LOVE

IN THIS SERIES:

The Timetraveller's Guide to Roman London
by Olivia Goodrich
Find out just why Rome's craziest emperors invaded cool, cruel
Britannia and built a city besides the Thames.
ISBN 1-904153-06-2

•

The Timetraveller's Guide to Medieval London
by Christine Kidney
Scratch, sniff and itch your way around the capital during its
smelliest period in history.
ISBN 1-904153-08-9

•

The Timetraveller's Guide to Shakespeare's London
by Joshua Doder
William Shakespeare is our greatest writer; read all about him,
his plays and the big bad city he lived and worked in.
ISBN 1-904153-10-0

•

The Timetraveller's Guide to Tudor London
by Natasha Narayan
See the terrible tyrants, cruel queens, con men and cutpurses
in Tudor London's dark, dingy and all too dangerous streets.
ISBN 1-904153-09-7

•

The Timetraveller's Guide to Victorian London
by Natasha Narayan
Get robbed and meet the snobs on a tour of Queen Vic's
top town.
ISBN 1-904153-11-9

In case you have difficulty finding any Watling St books in your local bookshop, you can place orders directly through

BOOKPOST
Freepost
PO Box 29
Douglas
Isle of Man IM99 1BQ

Telephone 01634 836000
email: bookshop@enterprise.net